The Stowaway Ghost

A ghostly tale

by Jillian Powell

Chapter One

When Sam woke up he was lying on a beach. His
hands were pressed into the wet sand. He smelled
salt and seaweed. He sat up and looked around.
The beach was empty. His handprints showed
where he had crawled up the shore. Then he saw
the wooden plank and remembered.

The plank from the ship had saved him. He had
held onto it like a raft when the ship went down.
He remembered the storm. He remembered
jumping, then the cold smack of the sea. After that,
he remembered nothing.

Was he the only one to survive? Had any of the
other boys from his school party reached the
island? If so, where were they?

Sam felt in his pocket. He felt his penknife, and his torch, and a piece of chocolate. He ate the chocolate hungrily. Then he stood up and looked slowly around. It was a beautiful beach. The sand was white. There were tall palm trees with coconuts on their branches. It was peaceful, too. The only sound was the waves crashing on the shore.

Then Sam saw the footprints. They were bigger than his. They ran up from the sea and across the wet sand. Then they stopped. There was just a hollow, as if someone had sat down. Sam was puzzled. Someone had walked up the beach, and stopped. But where had they gone? Perhaps they had turned back – but there were no footprints going the other way. They just stopped, suddenly, in the middle of the beach.

It didn't make sense. Someone had walked up the beach from the sea. Then they had just vanished into thin air. But Sam knew one thing. There was someone else on this island.

Chapter Two

Sam knew that he must make a shelter, and find some food to eat. For a while, he forgot about the footprints. He cut big palm leaves and long creepers from the forest. He made a frame of sticks and tied them together with creepers. Then he laid the palm leaves over the frame. That should keep out the sun and the rain.

Once or twice Sam thought he heard sounds in the forest. "It was probably just the wind in the trees," he thought. Then he heard the crackle of twigs underfoot. He remembered the footprints. There might be someone else nearby. There might be wild animals on the island, looking for something, or someone, to eat. He was beginning to scare himself.

He tried to keep busy looking for food. He used his penknife to split open a coconut and drank its milk. Then he found some big fruits that were orange and juicy inside.

The sun was going down. It was getting dark. A ghostly white moon was rising above the sea. Its light shone across the white sand. Then Sam saw it. Someone was sitting on the beach! The figure sat hunched in a ball. It was the colour of the moon, ghostly and white. It had no shadow and the moon seemed to shine right through it.

Sam watched, shivering, as the figure rose. It was
as if the moonlight had brought it to life. It began
to move slowly up the beach, towards the forest.
Sam saw its silvery light flicker between the trees,
and then vanish. He crept into his shelter and hid
his head under a pillow of palm leaves.

Chapter Three

When Sam woke up, he wondered if the white figure on the beach had been a dream. He soon found out it wasn't. Footprints in the sand led into the forest, where the figure had vanished. It was bad enough being shipwrecked ... but with only a ghost for company?

Sam knew he had to get off the island. He had an idea. If he lit a fire, a ship would see the smoke or flames. He spent all day gathering wood. He piled it up on the beach in a huge bonfire. He had heard that you could make a fire by rubbing sticks together. Sam took two sticks and began to rub.

He rubbed and rubbed, and sometimes a red spark flickered … then died. It was hopeless. And it was getting dark. The moon was beginning to shine on the beach again. Sam had almost given up when there was a sudden rush of wind. Something swept over the sticks, and the fire leaped into life. Sam fell back as the ghost swooped back and forth, fanning the yellow flames.

"Who … what are you?" he stammered. The ghost hovered, then wrote in the sand.

"A stowaway? You were a stowaway on our ship?" The ghost nodded.

"Where are you from?" Sam asked. This time the ghost drew in the sand. It was a picture of a pub, with a sign of a bull's head.

The ghost wrote that it had once been a boy, a bit older than Sam. It had haunted the pub for two hundred years. But it was boring, haunting the same place year after year … especially when you were no good at walking through walls, or making things move, or scaring people. The ghost had stowed away to find adventure. Now, like Sam, it was shipwrecked.

"Cheer up," Sam found himself saying. "Now you have helped me light a fire, another ship will see it and rescue us. You can stow away again."

The ghost sat hunched on the beach. The moon made it glow with a white light.

"I can only see you in moonlight," Sam said. The ghost nodded. "You will have to let me know where you are, when it's daylight. We'd better be friends. There's only us, you see, on the island."

Chapter Four

Shipwrecked on an island with only a ghost for company. Or so Sam thought. The next day, he found out he was wrong.

He had decided to explore the other side of the island. The ghost came with him, dropping coconuts every now and then to show him where it was. Suddenly, Sam stopped. There was a flag in the middle of the beach, made from a stick and a T-shirt. Sam knew that T-shirt anywhere. It belonged to Leo, the school bully.

"Well, well, well. What have we here?" A voice boomed down from the trees. "Of all the miserable creeps to end up on my island. A wuss called Sam."

"I'm not a wuss. And it's not your island," Sam said boldly. Leo swung lower in the tree.

"I think you'll find it is," he said with a nasty grin. "It seems like there's just the two of us, Sammy boy. And I'm in charge here so you can do as I say. You can start by fetching me some fruit."

"Fetch your own fruit!" Sam shouted.

Leo jumped down from the tree and held up his fists. "Want to fight?"

"No, I don't." Sam stopped. He could hear a rustling in the trees above Leo. A long creeper was being lowered, towards him. It looked like a cowboy's lasso.

"Scared Sam? You should be ..." Leo made towards him, but the lasso caught round his legs. He fell flat on his face on the sand.

"What the ...?"

Sam tried to hide his laughter.

"I don't want to fight, Leo," he said. "Just leave me alone. I'll stay on my bit of the island until we're rescued. You stay on yours." He turned to go.

"You'll be sorry!" Leo called after him.

Chapter Five

Sam couldn't believe he was doing this. It was the middle of the night, and he was giving a ghost lessons. In being scary.

"Hold your arms out. That's right. Now sort of wave them about. That's good! Much more scary."

The ghost looked pleased.

"Do you want to have a go at the tree again?" Sam asked.

The ghost had told him it wanted to be able to walk through walls. There were no walls on the island, but Sam had the idea that a tree might do. He told the ghost to start with the small trees, then work up until it could walk through the biggest tree on the island. Right now, the ghost kept smacking straight into the tree trunk, then holding its nose.

"Try it more slowly," Sam said. "That's it! Look, your arm is coming out the other side!"

"Talking to yourself now, loony tune?" It was Leo. Sam swung round.

"I thought I told you to keep to your side of the island," he said quietly.

"And I thought I told you that I was in charge here," Leo sneered.

29

"What's this?" Leo had found Sam's shelter. "This your poxy shelter?"

Leo kicked the shelter.

"It's rubbish! It will fall down any minute."

"Leave it, Leo!"

Sam could see the ghost, hovering behind Leo in the shadows.

"Leo," he said quietly. "Do you believe in ghosts?"

"Ghosts?" Leo snorted. "Yeah, sure. And there's one right behind me now, yeah?"

"Well, actually ..." Sam's words tailed off. The ghost was raising its arms spookily, right above Leo's head.

"Look, Fish-face. You can't scare me with a load of nonsense about ghosts," Leo said. "Ghosts are for wimps."

Sam saw the ghost rubbing its hands. He could tell it was working on a plan.

Chapter Six

The next night, there was a full moon. The whole
island shone with white moonlight. Sam had never
seen the moon look so big or so round. The ghost
seemed excited, as if it wanted to show
Sam something.

"This had better be good," Sam said, as he followed
it into the woods. This island was making him do
crazy things, he thought.

They reached a clearing and the ghost sat down on a log. It seemed to be waiting for something. Sam sat down too. They didn't have long to wait. Soon, small dancing lights began to appear in the sky. It reminded Sam of a laser show he had once seen at home. But when he looked more closely, he saw they were not lights.

They were flittering birds and bats. At least, they had the shape of them, but they were just ghostly shadows. Every time they flapped their wings, a shower of the colours they had once had rained down – dazzling blues, deep crimsons and bright yellows.

Just then, a ghost monkey swung out of a tree branch. Sam saw that even the tree was a ghost tree. He could see right through its trunk and on its branches were ghosts of leaves. They looked like the skeleton leaves you sometimes found in winter.

Sam realised that he was looking at the ghosts of every bird, animal and tree that had ever lived on the island.

"Does everything have a ghost then?" Sam asked the ghost. The ghost nodded, as if he thought everyone knew that. But the show only lasted while the moon was high in the sky. As soon as it began to sink, the dancing lights began to fade. Sam felt sleepy so they headed back. But there was one more surprise in store. Someone had smashed up his shelter.

Chapter Seven

That night, Sam slept on the beach. He woke to find
footprints going up and down the sand. The ghost
had been working on a plan all night. Then Sam
saw footprints heading towards Leo's camp.

Over on the other side of the island, Leo had been
doing some washing. He had washed his T-shirt
and shorts, and even his trainers. He had fixed up a
washing-line using a long tree creeper. Everything
was drying nicely. There was only one problem.
One of his trainers had gone missing from the line.
Leo had spent most of the day hunting for it. He
gave up, and went back to his shelter to get
something to eat. Then he saw the other trainer was
missing too.

"It's that nerd Sam," Leo thought. "He's come to get his own back for last night. Well, I'll show him who's boss on this island."

The sand burned his feet as he set out towards Sam's part of the island. He had to cross the forest to reach it. That meant taking care not to step on any creepy-crawlies.

Then he saw his trainer, lying under a tree. Perhaps an animal had carried it off after all. He went to pick it up. Then something odd happened. The trainer jumped out of reach. Leo blinked. He tried again. But now the trainer was hopping round and round the tree. And there was the other one, dancing in step.

Leo started to feel scared. Then he saw his T-shirt. It was hanging high up in a tree. He started to climb towards it. He reached out, but the T-shirt jerked away. It began dancing in step with the trainers, making an eerie sort of figure. Leo's heart was beginning to race.

He ran back to the washing-line, and his shorts had gone, too. "This is mad," Leo thought. "I must have heatstroke or something. Clothes can't move." He heard leaves crackle underfoot, and then he saw it. A figure was darting towards him. It wore his clothes and his trainers. It was himself, without a body. Leo began running. He had to get help. He had to find Sam.

Chapter Eight

"Oh sure," Sam said. "I expect it's the island ghost. He's always playing tricks. It upsets him, you see. When people don't believe in ghosts."

Leo was standing in front of him, in his boxer shorts, still shaking. Sam had never seen him look so white or so scared.

"So … if you do believe in them, in ghosts I mean, he leaves you alone?" Leo asked him.

"Well, it takes a bit more than that," Sam said. "You have to bring him presents. Things like coconuts and fruit, and nice shells and things."

"Okay," Leo nodded. "I'll start looking now."

Every day, Sam and the ghost found more gifts from Leo. Pearly shells, juicy coconuts, baskets of fruit. It made living on the island much easier. Leo seemed a bit more relaxed too. However, he had moved his shelter closer to Sam's and he still didn't dare to put on his clothes.

Then late one afternoon, Sam was sharing a coconut with the ghost when he saw a ship in the distance. It got bigger and bigger. It was coming towards the island.

"This is it," Sam said to the ghost. "We're going to be rescued."

"Stowaway?" the ghost wrote in the sand.

"Sure!" Sam said. "Just stay close behind me."

"Come on, lads!" the sailor said, helping them aboard. "Just the two of you?"

"Yes, just us," Leo said.

Sam followed behind him. Just two – and one stowaway ghost, he smiled to himself.